The power of
POSITIVITY

Controlling Where
the Ball Bounces

Cornell Thomas

FOREWORD

If there is one thing that we have learned in working toward improving our own lives and those we serve, is that there is great power in having a positive outlook on life. Whether you are going through a rough spot, or hoping to take your already awesome life to the next level, the stories, principles, and concepts contained in this book will serve as your inspiration.

Through the process of writing our book, we had the pleasure of meeting and getting to know Cornell Thomas. We always have room in our life for people of character and people who share our vision of inspiring others to pursue a better life. We connected instantly and remain in touch to this day. His energy and passion for life and for helping others is what we enjoy the most. Cornell is sincere and authentic. He doesn't just write about being positive, he is positive. Just by being around him you palpably feel his deep desire to share his message. He shares positivity with those he coaches; in his blog, on Twitter, and anywhere else he can find an ear. More importantly, he shares with more than just words; his actions are a living example of what living a positive life looks like.

The principle of a positive mental attitude is not new. It is time tested and universal. This book hits the spot, by presenting positivity in a fresh, new, and relatable way. Coach Cornell does a masterful job of teaching important principles in while at the same time entertaining and motivating the reader. This book can be read cover to cover, or if you are in need of specific inspiration, you can read that chapter individually. It doesn't matter the order it is read, it only matters that you embrace the concepts and practice them in your own life, and you too can be on your path to the life you dream of and deserve.

In Oola,

Dr. Dave Braun and Dr. Troy Amdahl

Co-Authors,"Oola: Find Balance in an Unbalance World"

www.OolaLife.com

CHAPTER 1 (SELF BELIEF)

1. THE POWER OF ME

There are times in our lives when we doubt ourselves; it's a natural human reaction. At some point as we grow up, we learn to be unsure. Go to an emergency room and you'll be amazed at how many kids you see scattered around. It takes a cast or two for us to question our invincibility, but eventually we do. I remember trying to do some type of bunk bed maneuver and having to get stitches on the bottom of my foot. After that my bunk bed routine was retired for good.

When we're kids, confidence doesn't have to be learned. Everything is new to us; we don't know the meaning of can't. We can do anything. I remember going out to the front stairs of my house equipped with just a garbage bag. I was convinced I'd be able to parachute down without a problem. Luckily for me there were only six stairs, or this story may have never happened.

It seems that the older we get, the less confident we become. When did we start becoming afraid of bugs or the dark? I can tackle one of those questions. I was about four years old and enjoying a jelly sandwich. (I don't like peanut butter–don't ask me why, I just don't) as I went to take another bite of this pile of purple sugar, a yellow jack decided it was also hungry.

Unfortunately, the yellow jack did not understand that although stinging me inside my mouth would not fill its belly, it would affect me for the next twenty or so years. I have run city blocks swinging wildly at bees, and I can only imagine what other people were thinking. Just recently I have learned to speed walk away, or swing lightly and side step my fear of bees.

This example illustrates that our experiences at a young age can change that swagger we possess when we're born. When we fail or hear that we're going to fail, we forget about the power of ME. The power of me is important in every aspect of life; it's amazing what can be accomplished when we actually believe in ourselves. On the other hand, not believing in ourselves can cripple us. Does the ultra marathon runner question if he can run 100 miles? I'm pretty sure he/she does. What makes them do it? It's the belief that no matter how difficult that task is they will pull through it.

My confidence has always been moderately high (no sarcastic comments please), but as I've gotten older, I have gotten even more confident. Now, are there times when I might doubt a decision I make? Of course, I'm human, but I also believe in myself. In fact, I think some people believe in me just because they see how I believe in myself. I'm a glass-is-half-full kind of guy. I've made a commitment to do the best with whatever cards I'm dealt because I've proven to myself that I can.

Believing in you isn't arrogance; it's common sense!! I was telling one of my players today how bright her future is going to be. I believe in her so much that I get goose bumps thinking of all the great things she'll accomplish in life. My only hope is that she sees the same thing inside of her that I do. I wish that not only for the players I work with, but for my friends, family, and whoever else I come across in my travels.

I have a goal sheet in my house, and I have about fifty things written down right now. I guess it could be called a goal or bucket list. Some of my goals have taken a little longer than I expected, but that doesn't make me question them or, more importantly, myself. I was raised on the adage "everything happens for a reason," so I believe that eventually they will happen.

My oldest brother Rob is a life coach. You can sit with him for ten minutes and immediately believe you can conquer the world. It's one of the things I love about him–it's his gift. I have a little bit of that gift as well, and it's what helps me motivate kids, friends, and family to do more than what they think is possible. I've always said if everyone had someone like Rob walking around with them every day imagine all the great things that could be accomplished on this earth. The funny thing is we all do walk around with that person; it's who we see in the mirror.

"Believe in yourself and others will follow suit"

SELF BELIEF – THE POWER OF ME

1) Imagine what you could do if you truly believed you could do it.

2) As long as you believe in yourself it doesn't matter who else does.

3) Every day there should be a better version of you in the mirror.

4) Anything is possible once you convince yourself that it is.

5) Finding yourself is easier when you don't have others looking for you.

6) You must figure out who you are to become who you want to be.

7) If you're not important in your own eyes you won't be in anyone else's.

8) The worst defeat is self defeat.

CHAPTER 2 (GIVING BACK) RAY

2. RAY

It would be tough for anyone to say in this day and age that they went through life without having anyone they looked up to, or had someone help them along the way. I was thinking about all the people throughout my life who have helped me on my own personal journey and who have also helped mold me into the person that I am today. Most were good influences; some were not. Those who were positive influences taught me attributes such as mental toughness, how to deal with adversity, and to believe in myself, even when others didn't.

There is one of my mentors, in particular, who continues to stick out in my mind. He was not the typical mentor (a mentor who is in a person's life for an extended period of time) such as a high school teacher, or a college football coach. My first mentor was with me for only about 6 hours. – Even though I saw this particular mentor from time to time in my life, there was really just one day that I will never forget. That one day I'm referring to ignited a spark in me that had significantly shaped my life at the time, and set me on a course that I'd remain on for more than a decade.

I started playing basketball at the age of 16 (which is really late in the grand scheme of things). Today, players begin actual 'training' in basketball as early as 5 years old– And, I am certain that some of these young players most likely possess better basketball skills than I did when I was a teenager. Growing up no one in my family played basketball. – So, when I decided to start trying I didn't have anyone to show me the ropes. So, I decided to be my own coach. I would walk down to the basketball court (which was about 2 miles away from my house) and throw the ball at the orange circle (which, only later, I found out was called the rim). I would pray from time to time that the ball would go in. – Needless to say, in the beginning I didn't have great success.

One Saturday during one of my "shooting sessions", it started to drizzle. If I left the court, I would have a 2-mile walk back home in the rain. – This was the age of pay phones; and, there was no way to call my mom to come and get me. – So, I decided that I might as well stay and continue to practice shooting a little more. – Across the street from the park I was shooting at, there were some houses; and, behind the houses, was just woods. Like out of a movie, my first basketball mentor magically appeared out of the woods and came walking towards the court. He introduced himself, and told me that his name was Ray. He asked me if I would mind if he showed me a couple of things. After I got over the fact that Ray somehow just appeared from the woods I couldn't believe that he was going to actually show me how to play basketball.

"There's no shame in asking for help from someone who has already traveled the road you yourself have yet to discover."

At that time, Ray was probably in his mid-thirties. He was about 5-foot-10, Asian, and looked completely different than the guys I watched playing basketball on TV. For the next 2 hours, Ray showed me everything he knew about shooting. He showed me how to hold the basketball; and, he talked to me about different basketball terminology. I found out that when I spastically dribbled to the basket and jumped to put it in the hoop that was called a "layup". I was amazed at how much patience he had with me. –I knew I wasn't very good; and, he did, too. But, he praised me for every little thing I did right. He never said anything negative when I missed . – He just showed me the right way to do it.

After Ray and I worked out, I practically glided home. I had this old run-down hoop that I tried to put up in my driveway; and, when I got back I continued to work on what Ray had shown me until there was no more light left to do so. Over and over, I could hear his voice as I shot, missed, watched the ball roll down the hill and then ran after it. I was hooked. – I had someone who <u>believed</u> in me. – I wanted to learn everything I could about the game of basketball; but, more importantly, I wanted to make sure that when Ray saw me next time he could tell that I had been working on what he had shown me.

About a week went by before I saw Ray again. I could tell that he saw some improvements in my game because he had the most genuine smile on his face. It was the same type of smile that teachers exhibit when a student who is struggling works really hard and gets an 'A' – or when a coach has a player he never thought would make the team – and, the next year, he or she does.

Sometimes people come in and out of our lives at the perfect time. I think the combination of Ray's patience and my desire to learn is what made it work. Ray doing such a selfless act for someone he had never met says a lot about the kind of person that he is. – That gentle push made me want to get better; and, in turn, it set me on a path that I might not have discovered until later on in life – if ever.

> *"Your impact on this world should be measured not by how much money you have made – but by how many people you have affected in a positive way."*

I saw Ray about only five more times after that. – This usually occurred during pick-up games; and, every time I would see him, he would tell me how much I had improved since the first time we met. Granted, I knew that I still had a long way to go; but, for him to say that meant a lot to me. – It also made me strive to get even better. As the years passed, I found out that Ray was a mail-man in the area, and that he lived right down the road from the court. (This helped to explain how he seemed to have initially just appeared out of nowhere.)

After I got out of high school and went to junior college, my basketball game started getting a lot better. By this time, I had a number of people whom I had come across who had helped me with my game at some point or another. But, I always found myself thinking about Ray and our first lesson. When I received a full scholarship to play at a four-year college, Ray again was on my mind. About a week after I got the scholarship, I was in the mall; and, as I was walking, I looked and saw Ray walking right towards me. – I couldn't believe it. – I hadn't seen Ray in 4 years; and, here he was right in front of me, just a week after I had received a full scholarship to play the sport he had taught me so long ago. I introduced myself right away (even though he remembered me) – and told him all about the scholarship. I was so excited; and, I don't know how much of my sentences were even coming out the right way. Ray smiled just like he did when we had first met; and, he told me, "I knew you would make it."

As I thanked him again and started walking away, I wondered if he knew the impact that he made in my life. I had no idea if he fully understood what those few sessions did for me. My life now consists of coaching and training kids. Every day, I now do what Ray had done for me. – Sometimes parents are amazed with how much time I put into working with their child, regardless of what his/her skill level is. A big reason is that I will never forget that someone did the same for me – and, that person will forever be in my heart because of it.

Maybe one day, one of the players I work with will say that I was the reason they got into coaching or training kids. – Or, maybe, one of them will just see me in the mall one day and thank me for changing their life. – I can't think of ANYTHING more rewarding than that!

GIVING BACK – RAY

1) Our natural instinct to survive should not override our ability to help one another.

2) Getting an opportunity to give back should be looked at as an honor not a chore.

3) Any day you can help someone improve is a day worth living.

4) There's no greater gift you can give someone else than giving them your time.

5) Good deeds without reward are done by those truest in heart.

6) There's nothing more inspirational than someone who inspires to be just like you.

7) You have to give back to get back, help others grow.

8) Give without wanting to get and get without forgetting who gave.

CHAPTER 3 (ADVERSITY)
THE FIGHTER WITHIN

✻ ✻ ✻

3. THE FIGHTER WITHIN

It was a normal day in Brazilian jiu jitsu class. We went through our warm up, drilled technique, and were now going to do some live training or "rolling" – to end the class. For those who don't know, Brazilian jiu jitsu is a martial art that focuses on ground fighting. It's one of the few martial arts where you can train or "spar" full throttle without severely injuring yourself. If you find yourself in a bad position, all you have to do is "tap" (which is like saying 'Uncle'). – This tells your partner to stop. I have been training at the same school in this particular martial art for about six years now. The people at the school are my extended family. – We hang out together; we know each other's kids, etc. In the past six years, I've "rolled" with some pretty amazing people, from world-renowned Brazilian jiu jitsu practitioners to famous instructors – but, <u>none</u> of this "rolling" compared to the training I had on this particular day.

The guy I "rolled" with was one of the toughest people I've ever met in my life; and, this wasn't because of his physical strength or even his jiu jitsu skill. The reason I say this is that on this day

– just like every other one for the last three-and-a-half years – he was fighting for his life.

I don't remember the exact day or time that I met Dan Copeland – or how many times before he was diagnosed with cancer that we "rolled" – but, what I do remember is coming to class and seeing him on the mats waiting to train that day. I knew Dan was undergoing chemo and was very weak physically. So, at first, I thought he would just watch the class (like he's done countless times in the past). To my surprise, he had on a "GI" (what we wear for jiu jitsu class), Then, just before we started training live, he asked me if I'd like to "roll" light with him. – So, we "rolled" for a six-minute round. – Dan would occasionally take a minute to catch his breath, but then would start right back up again and continue to train. – That day, I learned a lot about the human spirit and mental toughness.

I thought about how many times I've heard people complain about being too tired or sore to train. Then, I thought back to the days when even I didn't want to, because my body didn't feel one-hundred-percent. After that day of training with Dan, I asked myself a question, "Can you just imagine the pain – both physical and mental – Dan has been going through for the last three-and-a-half years?" I immediately felt shame and anger and decided that I would never take another day for granted.

After our "roll", Dan thanked me for training with him; and, we gave each other a hug. All the guys at my jiu jitsu school call me "Big C" – but, I can't put into words how small I felt after leaving the school that day. – It would be the last time I would ever see Dan again. – After a long battle with cancer that lasted three-and-a-half years, Dan passed away a couple of days ago. – You never know when it might be the last time you see someone; and, I can't believe that God allowed me to be with Dan on the mats for that last time.

A month ago, I heard that Dan's condition was getting worse and that he was going to stop doing chemotherapy. – I wrote Dan a message, letting him know how much he has inspired me to continue to fight for what I want, and to never give up. My only prayer was that, hopefully, someone was able to read that message to him before he passed on. They say that people never get the flowers, when they can still smell them; and, that is so true. Dan has left a legacy that will never be forgotten and that will live through his family and friends.

I lost a family member, but gained inspiration for the rest of my years on this earth. Thank you, Dan Copeland, for showing me what real toughness is all about!

ADVERSITY – THE FIGHTER WITH IN

1) Prepare for the worst but hope for the best.

2) The light at the end of the tunnel is seen by those unfazed by the darkness that surrounds them

3) What breaks you makes you, learn from tough times.

4) It's not the setback that determines your future; it's how you recover from it.

5) It's amazing how much time is wasted complaining about a bad situation instead of trying to actually fix it.

6) You're only as strong as the last obstacle you've overcome

7) When times are tough think outside of yourself, remember it could always be worse.

8) When it all hits the fan turn the fan off

CHAPTER 4 (MOTIVATION)
THE VOICE

✧ ✧ ✧

4. THE VOICE

I don't know when it first started. I'm not sure how old I was or the first time I heard it. All I know is that once I heard it that first time, it never left. Some days it's not as loud as others, but it's always there. The voice told me that getting cut from Varsity as a junior was only going to make me stronger. It also told me that I would get a basketball scholarship no matter what anyone else said. When I was running sprints and felt like quitting, it told me to get mad and get through it. It came to me when I thought it wasn't there or paying attention anymore.

It let me know that coaching is what I needed to do, because although my dreams were great, there was a bigger calling out there for me. During the season my team didn't win a single game I thought it left for good, but it returned when it was over, telling me to get on the phone and recruit more players, go to more coaching clinics, and change my attitude. I had no idea if opening up my own business would ever work, but the voice didn't care about that; it just cared about what steps I needed to take for it to come to fruition.

There's a voice we all have inside our heads, and it's very powerful. It's the one that tells you either to work out or open the bag of Doritos. When the voice is optimistic, there's no limit to what you can do, because the voice makes you feel that you can do anything you put your mind, heart, and soul into. When the voice is pessimistic the opposite occurs: now you believe there's nothing you can do; you don't look for challenges; you can't deal with adversity, and nothing feels like it will work out in your favor.

"Hear what's being said, especially when it's your own voice urging you to get through the tough times"

I will not allow myself to break down. I will not allow myself to quit. I will not allow myself a second of self pity or self doubt. Instead I will do the exact opposite. If you repeat that mantra over and over in your head, how can you fail? How could you wake up and not feel confident taking on the day?

There have been so many times in my life where the voice has gotten me through the rough patches. Without thinking about it, I hear it when I start to feel overwhelmed or when I think it's going to be impossible to do something. It takes a while to develop, but once you do, it's something that can save your life. Over 30,000 Americans commit suicide every year. Where is their voice? What are they hearing? They're hearing that it's hopeless, that there's nothing they can do to change their current situation, it's telling them to quit and they do. If only their voice would convince them that their lives alone are a reason not to leave this earth.

For the past two weekends we've been holding tryouts for our travel basketball teams. Kids from as young as nine to as old as seventeen compete against other players to make our basketball teams. Over 280 kids tried out, but we could only keep 180 of them. All I've been thinking about is the voices of the kids that didn't make the cut. What message is it saying to them? Is it saying try another sport? Is it saying that the people who evaluated them obviously don't know what they're talking about? Is it making them look at the kids who made the team and wonder how "they" made it and not them? Or, has the voice already gotten them in the driveway shooting jump shots. Maybe it told them that by next year, they have to be better. I hope it's the latter. I hope the same voice that I heard in high school telling me to get better is relaying the same message to them.

The best thing about the voice is that you can control it. It's up to you what messages you send yourself. If used the right way it can be a very powerful tool in your life. Listen to the messages you're sending yourself; if all is well, then keep doing what you're doing; if not maybe it's time to change your voice.

MOTIVATION – THE VOICE

1) You can waste time doing what you hate or make time doing what you love.

2) If you never try you'll never know

3) The voice you hear pushing you should be your own

4) Motivate yourself and others won't have to

5) You can't finish a race unless you start it

6) Go after what you want because it's rarely going to go after you.

7) Sometimes the best motivation is simply wanting to be better than you were yesterday.

8) Never waste a minute regretting what you could have done.

CHAPTER 5 (MAKING AN IMPACT) TOP 3

✩ ✩ ✩

5. Top 3

I was at a coach's clinic this summer and the speaker was talking about the effect that coaches have on their players' lives both on and off the court. Obviously this topic was not something new to me because I have coached for a decent amount of years, and I have seen the effects first hand. What struck a chord with me though was the question the speaker asked all of us in the audience. He asked us if we were in any of our players' top three. At first I didn't know what he meant by that and most of the other coaches in attendance had the same puzzled look I did. The speaker then went on to elaborate a little more and explained that the list consisted of people that influenced your players lives. I was floored by that question because honestly I never really put too much thought into it. I immediately starting thinking to myself, am I on anyone's list?

I thought a top three list would most likely consist of just parents and siblings. I know that my mom is obviously on my list along with one of my brothers but who would I put as that third person? I have been influenced and continue to be influenced by so many different people as I go through life. I hear amazing stories all the time about people that overcome adversity and accomplish great things. That's why my third person doesn't jump out at me right away. I know for a fact that there are definitely players that I have had on my team that wouldn't put me in their top three hundred. One's that I have worked extremely hard and never quite got it. I think another reason I might not know if I'm on a list is because to me it's kind of cocky to assume. I'm just a regular human being like anyone else. Obviously it would be an honor but I could never think of myself being on someone's top three.

Yesterday I got a text message from a former player that I haven't talked to in a long time. A great kid that I worked pushed extremely hard when he played for me. He only played for one year because of an injury but the season he played I was on him every day about working hard and staying focused. I'll never forget one preseason six a.m. workout where he wanted to quit. We were in the middle of running lines (down and backs full court) and he approached me and said he couldn't do it anymore. He told me that he had to work and couldn't play basketball this season. Usually (especially during preseason) I wouldn't of cared, I would've said goodbye and let him walk out the gym but with this particular kid I knew had it in him to push through the pain. I told him that if we were doing any other activity besides running he wouldn't be quitting (in not that nice of language) then I walked away. After a couple of minutes I saw him standing by the door, the next thing I know he s back on the baseline trying to push through it. I started running it with him, and then one of my assistants started running with us, and then the whole team is taking turns helping him get through the lines. It's one of those moments as a coach that you live for. A kid making a breakthrough and pushing past something he once thought was impossible. So yesterday in his text message he told me that he was doing well and working on his degree, he thanked me for everything that I've done for him and told me how much my words had inspired him to overcome adversity. Anyone that knows me knows that I'm horrible at taking compliments. It's the only thing that makes me shy and thank god this kid couldn't see me because I was speechless and may or may not of had a tear in my eye.

That night another player that I haven't talked to in about a year wrote something on my face book page. Now this player I kicked off the team and was probably harder on him than almost anyone I've ever had. The funny thing is even when he played at another school whenever I saw him we always had good conversations. He wrote; **"This great man he is the reason I'm getting my degree and coaching now he's all about helping others getting better I hope to follow in his footsteps."** Again I was blown away and immediately told him to contact me soon so we could catch up.

You never know what kind of effect you have on someone until they tell you or you physically see it. Out of all the players that I have coached I would have never picked the two that I just talked about to have me in their top three hundred let alone their top three. I tell my mom all the time how much of an effect she has had on who I am today. I think it's important that she knows this. I can't describe the feeling I got when I read my former players messages, it made me feel like everything I taught them sunk in, and it didn't matter when it only mattered that it did.

Who's on your top three? Whose top three are you on? If you're on no one's top three what's the reason? People that give back will always be on someone's list somewhere. It doesn't have to be material possessions, it could be your time, it could be a shoulder to cry on, or it could be advice. Whatever the case may be try your best to be in someone's top three, it's more rewarding then you could ever know.

IMPACTING OTHERS – TOP 3

1) Leadership isn't a part time job it's a full time responsibility.

2) Your eyes can only see so far, trust your heart when they fail you.

3) Be a problem solver not a problem maker.

4) Every wrong answer is an opportunity to find the right one.

5) Sometimes what you have to do is more important than what you want to do.

6) Opportunity has to be seen before it can be taken advantage of.

7) Live in the moment not the memory.

8) The bigger picture can't be seen by those without vision.

CHAPTER 6 (LEGACY) LETTER TO BOBBY

☆ ☆ ☆

6. LETTER TO BOBBY

When I was about fifteen years old, I thought about writing you a letter. I wanted to tell you all the things that had happened in the 11 years since you passed away. For whatever reason it never got completed, and I never had the thought to do it again until about four days ago. In July members of your immediate family are organizing an event in Passaic NJ to honor all the work you did for the community through your "Doin it in the park" events and the countless hours you put in helping the youth in the city. I hardly knew you before you passed, but the older I get, the more I learn about the man you were and the legacy you left behind.

I grew up with some memories of you, but mostly stories. For example, mom told me how hard you fought her to call me Cornell and not Nelly. I want to thank you for that; I couldn't imagine going through life as Nelly. One of my favorite memories occurred when I was about three years old. It was Christmas, and when I rolled out of bed I stepped on a toy. The whole room was filled with toys, and I remember trying to figure out how they all got there. When I went to your bedroom, you and mom were both fast asleep. To this day I still remember some of those toys. I can't imagine how long it must have taken you to put all the toys in the room while two over-anxious boys slept. As I got older I found out that not only did 544 Gregory Ave have a secret Santa, but so did much of the city of Passaic thanks to your toy drives and efforts in the community.

Tomorrow is father's day, and like each one before it, I don't have anyone to hug or thank. Mom did a great job being both parents, but I always wonder what it would have been like if you were still around.

I look at my path in life, and I'm amazed at how I ended up where I am today. Growing up, I never wanted to be a police officer like you and Rob. In fact, I didn't really know what I wanted to do. Mom encouraged us to do what we loved, but I wasn't sure what that was. During my junior year, I found basketball and fell in love with something that helped shape me into the man I am today. When I would see my friends' fathers at our games, I would wonder what it would be like if you were there. Truth be told I was horrible for the first four years of my basketball career, so I don't know how much you would have actually wanted to see. Luckily, I have mom's drive and your energy. Thanks to those two things I was able to improve drastically, and I eventually get a scholarship to play college basketball in North Dakota. I got my degree, and found my wife all in the same place.

Our paths up to this point couldn't have been more different. After I got a contract to play professionally overseas, I got injured. Everyone tells me how tough you were, and you obviously know how tough mom is; I can only thank god that I inherited some of that toughness. After my injury, I took 3 days off before getting back in the gym. I could have let it break me, but I know that's not what Thomas's do. Even though I was able to work my way back, an opportunity came to coach basketball instead of play it. My wife Melissa (who you'd love) was the first person to say I'd be good at it, and then I had to convince myself to believe her.

My first coaching job was as a head coach with no experience at all. It wasn't until I started coaching that I realized what I was meant to do in life. Mom always tells us that everything happens for a reason, and I think the reason I got injured was to lead me to this profession; once I started coaching and then training kids I saw this for my own eyes. The picture that I put on this letter is one of my favorite ones of you. It was taken during a community cleanup project you were doing in Passaic. You can tell that you're leading the charge. Not only did you have adults cleaning up, but you also had kids doing the same. There are adults that come up to Romont in Passaic all the time and tell him how much you influenced their lives. You've been gone for over thirty years, but people still talk about all the great things you did for the community.

I started a basketball training business, and we have over 300 kids that participate in our basketball programs. My goal with each one is to be a positive influence for them, and teach them life lessons on and off the court. If I could impact one person's life like you did thousands I would consider it a success.

I visited you for the first time since you passed away last year. The first thing I felt was anger. I couldn't believe that someone that did so much for people didn't have a big headstone, but then

I realized that you wouldn't have wanted it any other way. You always thought about others before yourself. You probably would have asked them to make Otto's (the person next to you) head-stone bigger before they did yours.

You influenced my life more than I can express, so I felt that I had to let you know somehow. If I could impact people the way you have, I know when it's time to leave this world I can in peace, as you probably did. I couldn't have asked for better parents; father's day is every day for me.

PUSHING YOURSELF – THE OTHER ME

1) You can't be a part time worker and expect full time result.

2) There's pain in getting better that's why so many don't improve.

3) Preparation for the fight is more important than the fight itself

4) You don't have to be the best to do your best.

5) If you're not willing to sweat you're not willing to win

6) Sometimes just trying harder is half the victory.

7) Repetition builds confidence, if you don't train, don't be upset with the results.

8) The will to win needs to be greater than the fear of losing.

CHAPTER 7 (SUCCESS) MUSICAL CHAIRS

✿ ✿ ✿

7. MUSICAL CHAIRS

This past week I was at a coach's clinic in Indiana. The clinic is run by one of the assistant coaches of the Boston Celtics and another long-time NBA assistant coach. Some of the brightest and most successful coaches in the country have spoken at this clinic in the past, so I make sure I attend every summer, no matter where it's held.

One of the speakers was a strength and conditioning guru, and he used a very interesting analogy. He was talking about levels of play and he compared competition to musical chairs. Now you all remember that cut throat game you played in school; you know the one where sitting in a chair meant you can legally injure someone with no repercussion. For the younger generation that might be too "guarded" to have played this game the premise is this. You put a bunch of chairs in a circle (one or two fewer than the number of people you start with) and when the music starts everyone walks in a circle around them, when the music stops everyone must find a chair to sit in. This is where the fun begins; someone is going to be left without one. If your butt is not in a seat when the music stops, you're eliminated from the game. Every round more chairs are taken away and so on and so on until there is one person left. Bottom line is this game can get pretty intense. Gender, age, and bloodline don't matter.

The speaker said that every level of basketball you go up there are fewer chairs and more people. I immediately connected with his words. We tell our kids all the time that the difference from middle school to high school is that there are more players and less opportunity to make a team. The same applies if you want to play in college. Now instead of going up against kids from your high school to make a team, you're going against kids from all over the country, and in some cases the world. Did you know that you're playing the game right now? I didn't until I realized that all these college coaches that were around me at the clinic had a similar goal to mine—to become a Division 1 Head Coach. True to the analogy, there are hundreds of thousands of coaches trying to find a seat, but there are only 345 seats to sit in.

I was in the middle of a game that I hadn't played since middle school without knowing it. The good thing is I'm preparing to win that game every day; for instance, I was preparing at the coaches clinic. The chairs represent opportunity, the music represents time. We all know that when opportunity knocks, we're sometimes just seconds from answering the door before it walks away. Musical chairs was my first lesson in coming up short.

I knew when I heard this analogy I was going to make it into a blog. As soon as I got back to New Jersey I used the same analogy for our kids at camp. I just feel it's so important for them to know that a spot on a team or an A on a paper or a perfect life isn't guaranteed. We live in a world where literally "the strong survive". The best students usually go to the best schools, the best athletes get scholarships, and the richest people usually get the best things out of life (materially). Competition is not a bad thing; in fact, I think it brings out the best in a lot of us, but imagine if you weren't aware that you were in one????

I know how cutthroat the world of college basketball is. I'm fully aware of how many coaches want the exact same job I do, and how hard they're working to get it. That's why I work so hard. That information drives me to run a camp on Monday, leave that night for Indiana, and sit in a classroom for eleven hours straight just learning. If I didn't go to the clinic this week, I would have missed not only that analogy (that I will use forever) but a ton of other useful information. The two hundred or so attendants would have beaten me to the chair, and I can't let that happen.

Understand that you're playing that game every day. Are you working towards something? Do you have a goal that more than just you wants? Are you waking up every day and doing everything in your power so that you're not the odd man out? When the music stops will your butt be in a seat??

SUCCESS – MUSICAL CHAIRS

1) To succeed without sacrifice is impossible.

2) If you're afraid to fail you'll never take the risk necessary to succeed

3) Every today is another opportunity to be better than yesterday.

4) Success is determined by how hard you're willing to work to obtain it

5) The fast track to success is usually filled with those that have already lost the race

6) Successful habits make successful people.

7) Embrace the pain of success not the comfort of failure.

8) Hold yourself accountable for your own success.

CHAPTER 8 (MENTAL TOUGHNESS) CAN'T

✮ ✮ ✮

8. CAN'T

There are plenty of colorful four letter words in the English language. I'm pretty sure that I have used a good amount of them throughout my coaching career. Out of all these words, the one that I" never use is the word can't. I have been a basketball coach and trainer for nine years, and my battle with can't happens every day. One of the hardest things for me as a coach is to get the word can't out of my player's vocabulary. If I asked you to run a marathon right now, what would you say? If you're not a runner, you'd most likely say, "I can't do that". It's a lot easier to say you can't do something than to actually try and find out if you can.

I try to put myself in situations where I have to fight can't. I might be lifting, or on a run, or doing jiu jitsu, and the next thing I know my mind is telling me that there's no way I can run another mile, do another set, or get out of a bad position. Replacing can't with can is a must if you ever want to break through your comfort zone. Players confuse being uncomfortable with not being able to do something. When we do sprints in practice the players that come in dead last throughout the whole training session somehow push through the last sprint when we inform them whoever comes in first is done. Weird how that works!

You hear the phrase "nothing is impossible." In a general sense that's true. Now, none of us have the ability to fly, or jump over tall building in a single bound, but if you look close enough there are lots of people doing the impossible every day. Inventions, medical discoveries, athletic feats that were said to be impossible become possible because there are those out there who don't allow can't into the picture. Remember when the four minute mile couldn't be broken? How about doing the hundred meter dash under ten seconds? Elite high school runners have broken the mile time under four minutes, and Usain Bolt just did the 100m in a world record 9.58 seconds. Thank god these men and women didn't have cant in their vocabulary.

Sometimes can't is really won't in disguise. I can't do another sprint means I won't do another sprint. I can't push through this last mile means I won't push through this last mile–instead I'm going to quit. This is the struggle for all of us. Why can't you accomplish your dreams? Maybe you have an I instead of the why in front of that last sentence. I love when people tell me I can't do something. It's not about me proving them wrong; it's about proving myself right. Every time I do, I believe in myself more and more. When I started a college basketball game, when I scored twenty points for the first time, when I made an all-conference team, when I got the basketball scholarship no one thought I could: I knew I'd be able to accomplish those feats if I worked hard enough, and once I did, it made me more confident and it made me believe in myself.

I'm big on writing my goals down on paper. It gives me an opportunity to look at them from time to time and see where I'm at. Did I give up and let can't stop me from accomplishing what I want? What have you tried to accomplish but quit because you didn't think it was possible? Did you ever revisit it and try again? Whenever I show kids basketball drills I find out which ones they like immediately. It's the ones where they look good doing it. Usually the drills they struggle with are the ones they stop practicing. They're thinking can't instead of can.

I just heard a story today about one of our parents. A couple of months ago he decided to start running to get in shape. I remember seeing him run that first day, and he did about a half mile or so–maybe less. Now, he's doing two. In another couple of months (knowing this guy), he'll be doing four or more. Imagine if he had stopped at a half mile?? He would have never found out what he could really accomplish, and that's what the word can't does. It bails us out. Well, I never tried it so I don't know if I could do it or not. The first time I tried to play guitar I couldn't believe how bad I sounded. I kept asking myself how do people make this instrument sound good. After a while it started to sound better, and eventually it got to the point where the animals didn't run away when I started playing. (Singing is another story).

Can't is the worst of all the four letter words so do yourself a favor and replace it with can!!

MENTAL TOUGHNESS – CAN'T

1) The little voice that tells you to quit is waiting for you to prove it wrong.

2) When you think you can't go one more step, take two just to prove yourself wrong.

3) Quitting becomes easy if you allow yourself to do it enough times.

4) You're toughest adversary is usually the one in the mirror.

5) If the mind quits the body will do the same, a strong mind can carry a weak body.

6) If you allow yourself to hear just the negative the positive will slowly become background noise.

7) You can't push past your limits without knowing them first.

8) Your mind can be your biggest asset or your worst enemy, choose wisely.

CHAPTER 9 (DEALING WITH OTHERS) SHAKING HANDS

✧ ✧ ✧

9. SHAKING HANDS

At some point in time someone somewhere decided that shaking hands would be the way that people would greet each other. Next thing you know everyone is doing it for centuries to come. Nowadays you can lose a job opportunity because of the way you shake hands on your interview. People get judged on their handshakes all the time. **"He had a dead fish handshake,"** that's the one where the other person doesn't squeeze; instead their hand just lays in yours. **"He gave me the Incredible Hulk,"** that's the handshake (mainly) amongst guys where the person thinks your hand is the grip machine down the shore and tries to break it with one squeeze. Whatever technique you do the handshake is very important when it comes to greetings and, for that matter, goodbyes.

I think it's safe to say that through the years that I have shaken thousands of hands. From teammates, to opponents, to faculty members, to friends, I have had my fair share of handshakes. Out of all of them though there is one that I will never forget, and the memory will stay with me for the rest of my life. It's a handshake that I forced myself to do, despite the fact that most people would've done the opposite.

My senior year in college was supposed to play out something like this: not only start but play forty minutes per game, lead the team in scoring and assists, win our conference, and then make a run at the national tournament. I had one year left, and the summer before my senior year I spent it playing with former and current NBA players, overseas players, and Division 1 players. I felt that all the time I put in getting better would pay off. No one worked as hard I did that summer (in my mind), and I sacrificed everything just to make sure that nothing would stop me from reaching my goals. Then something happened.

The year before I had to take a medical redshirt because I broke a bone in my left foot. It was tough sitting out the whole season, but I did my best cheering the guys on and trying to lead by being vocal and giving advice to those who needed it. At the start of my senior year the players had to pick the captains for the upcoming season; I was picked as one along with another senior. Our head coach was a white guy from Idaho who never played above the JV level in high school. He was about thirty-two years old and for whatever reason didn't care for any of the "inner city" players he recruited; in his mind, "inner city" meant that we–the six minorities on the team–were from outside of North Dakota.

I had been through so much up until that point with basketball that it never crossed my mind that maybe the season I dreamed about wouldn't happen. The players picked me as their captain, I knew I worked harder than everyone else, and I was the best player at my position, hands down. Somehow none of that mattered once the season started. Despite practicing at least six hours every day on the basketball court, I was relegated to the bench. I couldn't understand it and neither could my team-mates. Guys would tell me to just keep playing hard and keep my head up. I was averaging around fourteen minutes per game and ten points per game. It got to the point where my teachers would come to games and ask what the coach had against me. I never stop playing hard, I never talked back, and I would never quit the game I love no matter how little I played.

By the middle of the season we were about two games under 500 and the team, which was very talented, was at a crossroads. Most guys weren't listening to the coach or were tuning him out completely. At two o'clock one morning, I got a phone call from coach saying that there would be a mandatory team meeting at nine that same day. No one knew what it was about, but he started calling guys into his office one by one. When it was my turn ,I could see that he had been up all night. His eyes had bags under them and were red like he had been crying. He then asked me if he should resign. I told him that the team wasn't responding to what he was saying and things needed to change (discipline etc). We then got to the subject of my playing time. He looked me in the eyes and told me that if I was on another team I would be averaging thirty points a game right now. The team he said was the number one team in our conference, they happened to have all black kids and one Native American player. I asked him how I could be a "star" on that team which was ranked in the country, and not even a starter on this one which was third to last in the same conference. No answer. After I left his office, some of the guys and I discussed the meeting and almost everyone said they told coach he should resign; even the North Dakota kids, who he liked a lot, said the same.

Ironically, that night we were playing a game against the same team coach said I would be a star on. As the first half ended I had yet to play. I figured my honesty was the reason for it. With six seconds left in the first half coach looked down the bench and told me to get in the game. I popped up, got in, ran down the court, and then it was halftime. We were down by eighteen and I didn't even question why he subbed me in at that point. In the second half I didn't play at all. So for the game I played six seconds. I talked to my girlfriend at the time and told her that he was trying to break me. He wanted me to quit and that was his way of doing.

The next day I flew home for Christmas break and told my mom everything that was going on. She told me that if he played me for thirty minutes or thirty seconds to make the best of it. When I got back to school I did just that. It got to the point where he had no choice but to play me. I was finishing games and when the newspaper asked about me during a big win he had no choice but to comment in a positive way. We had a home game and despite playing only sixteen minutes I almost had a triple double (18pts 8reb 8asst), and we won. After the game my coach didn't even say good game. He walked past me as I was being interviewed. I never said anything negative about him to anyone, and despite the cold shoulder I still got to play the game I love.

After the season ended the boosters had a luncheon for all senior athletes from each team. The captains had to go up and say a short speech. I talked about how when I came to North Dakota

I thought there were going to be tumbleweeds rolling across the street. I shared my first national geographic sighting (when we say buffalo on our way to a game in a field) and I also told them how great an experience it was coming to school there. My coach was sitting in the audience as I said these things. Now I could have gone into everything that went wrong, but instead I talked about the good things. A couple of days later the newspaper did a story that discussed how our season went wrong and questioned my coach's decisions. I never talked to them about anything nor would I. I knew this experience would make me stronger and I was certain I would play pro basketball despite everything that happened.

We had no banquet after the season, so I didn't hear from or see coach for the next three months. In the meantime, I worked out, went to the gym, and took care of my school work. My plane ticket home was for the second week of May. The day before I was supposed to leave I was in the gym shooting when the most unexpected thing happened. As I was walking out coach jogged up to me and said he was looking for me all over campus. That alone was surprising; we hadn't talked in months, and I was on my way home tomorrow. What could he possibly say to me?

He went on for about a half hour about how he messed up. He said I should have been starting the whole season that he played me wrong; he talked about how I was a hard worker and a good kid. He kept going on about my character and how my grades were also a reflection of who I was. As I stood there, I looked him in the eyes the whole time. He couldn't meet my eyes more than a couple of times, because his were watering. I kept thinking to myself after all this time you choose to apologize now? My senior year was over, my college career was done and now he is having an epiphany? I was silent the whole time he talked–I didn't say one word–and then finally at the end he put his hand out for me to shake it. I had so many emotions at that point, anger being one of them, and there was his hand in front of me. I was thinking that he took my senior year away from me and now he wanted forgiveness. Something made me reach my hand out and shake his. It looked like he was going to collapse when I did. I could see that he felt relieved that I shook his hand and didn't punch him. The next day I went home and went about working out and trying to improve.

The next year I got a call from one of my teammates that was still playing for the college. He said that coach was completely different. He was laughing with the players, hanging out with them, and even lifting weights with everyone (he was a little on the puny side). The one that got me was the fact that he recruited another kid from New Jersey. As the years went by he had more and more "inner city" kids come in. About two years after I left they got to the national tournament, one of those years actually making it to the elite 8.

I forgave a man that realized he made a mistake. I would like to think just like he helped me (motivation wise) put all the extra hours in the gym, I helped him see that what he was doing wasn't the right thing. If I would have acted in a negative way when he went to shake my hand who knows what could have happened. Maybe everything he thought about me in the beginning would have been true in his mind. Maybe he would have been the same way for his whole coaching career and never changed.

It's easy to be angry, it's easy to hold grudges, but it's hard to put your ego aside sometimes and realize that we are all human and humans make mistakes. I imagined myself being coach and how hard it must have been to swallow his pride and say sorry. The whole situation helped make me who I am today and for that I will always owe him.

DEALING WITH OTHERS – SHAKING HANDS

1) Don't change who you are to change someone's opinion of who they think you are.

2) Never mistake the people who matter in your life with the ones that don't.

3) Never doubt yourself others will do that for you.

4) Be aware of people without direction, they're usually the ones getting other people lost.

5) The more bridges you burn the fewer roads you can travel.

6) Negative people are the best recruiters, don't take the bait.

7) It's hard to dream big if you let others make you feel small.

8) Your environment only shapes you it doesn't make you.

CHAPTER 10 (POSITIVITY) MAGNETS

10. MAGNETS

I'm not sure of the exact day but I do remember it was in elementary school when I first experienced magic. My friend Harold had somehow made a paper clip move around his desk without using his hands. As me and my classmates looked on in astonishment Harold just smiled at us like he was David Blaine levitating in front of an amazed crowd. After about thirty seconds of this Harold (unlike Mr. Blaine) revealed the mystery. He produced a magnet from underneath his desk. I couldn't tell you what happened the rest of class because I was trying to see how many paper clips this mysterious new toy could attract at the same time. I'm pretty sure this was during math class. (Thank you Harold for helping me hate math)

It was my first experience with how magnets worked. I was fascinated by their ability to draw things towards them. A couple of months later my science teacher brought in a bunch of different magnets for us to play with. Some were small like the one Harold was using, and others were about the size of a ruler. I was so fascinated with how powerful the bigger ones were I kind of blocked out how they actually worked. I would hear the words "atoms" and "magnetic fields" in the background while I wondered what size magnet I would need to attract a car to it. (This was before kids got diagnosed with A.D.D. for not paying attention)

Flash forward about twenty or so years later and I learned about a different type of magnet the *"law of attraction"*. The law of attraction basically means that *"like attracts like"*. This lesson wasn't taught in a classroom setting. A friend of mine told me about a book called "The Secret", and in this book the law of attraction was discussed throughout it. What I didn't realize at the time was this law was something that I've been experiencing my whole life, I just didn't realize it.

Actual magnets have a scientific explanation for the reason they attract things. The law of attraction is a belief. It's a feeling. There is no scientific data that can explain how or as I would later find out why it works. I was on my way to Las Vegas for a basketball clinic. I had just left my coaching job at Sussex County College without another job in place. At the end of the season I just felt like I needed to move on. I had a job interview at Blair Academy set up for when I got back, but I had no idea how it would go.

On the plane ride I started reading about how in the law of attraction whatever you feel is basically what you attract. So if you're a positive person usually positive things happen to you and vice versa. I had a gut feeling about leaving my current job, I could have still taught classes there, but I didn't want to. I wanted to leave completely; I was basically jumping off a tightrope with no idea if there was a net below to catch me. The more I read the book the more sense it made. I was halfway through it when the plane landed. The book started giving different examples of the law. Like how when you're thinking about someone the next thing you know they text you, or when you're wishing you had more money you find a five dollar bill in the dryer. All these things have happened to me more times than I could remember.

The book had my full attention; it was all I could think about. The law of attraction was amazing and a little scary which drew me in even more. I went down to the pool with a friend of mine later that day and as we walked around this guy was reading the same book with the cover blatantly facing us. When I got on the plane to go home the person next to me saw the book cover from my bag and we got into a two hour discussion about it.

I started to realize that I could attract great things just by staying positive. The next day I had the interview and it went great. I got the job at Blair, and then on the way home got an email that secured a second job at a basketball facility. In a total of an hour I was going to make twice as much as I did the previous year. I was a believer before but after that I was "all in".

I feel we are all magnets. You meet some people that always seem to have that rain cloud over their heads. They go through setback after setback until eventually they feel there's no hope for things to change. On the other hand there are others who seem like the "luckiest" people in the world. Good fortune happens to them on a daily basis, and it keeps happening. If you believe in energy you believe in the law of attraction. There are two types of energy positive and negative. Sometimes you get every green light on the way to work, and sometime you hit every red. Think about that.

The power of positivity

You can think positive all the time and still have some bad things happen. The key is how you react when bad things do. I tell people all the time that I don't have "bad days" I only have "bad thoughts" from time to time. If I let that thought linger, eventually it will end up becoming a bad day. It's a lot easier for me to deal with one thought than a whole day of things going wrong. Once you feel the thought come up, extract it from your thoughts and start to think more positive. You have a double shift you have to work on the weekend? O.k. that might stink, but at least you're getting paid for it. The job you wanted didn't hire you? Maybe that wasn't the perfect fit for you, and just maybe a better job is right around the corner.

Positive thinking produces positive results. Make sure your magnet is focused on the good, not the bad.

POSITIVE THINKING – MAGNETS

1) Expect more and you'll never settle for less.

2) Positive energy is sustained through positive thought.

3) Anything is possible once you convince yourself that it is.

4) You are what you attract.

5) Happiness is a state of mind, you control your happiness.

6) If you don't believe in yourself no one else will.

7) Don't waste time being anyone else but yourself.

8) Don't let a bad thought become a bad day.

BONUS CRAIG

I come from a fairly big family. I have three brothers, one sister, two half-brothers and one half-sister. Although my half-brothers and half-sister didn't live in the same house, we still have the same blood that runs through our veins.

Each of my family members, at some point in time, has served as a big influence in my life. My oldest half brother, Rob, is still to this day one of my most-treasured mentors. He's the person whom I go to for advice or direction when I'm unsure of something. My oldest brother, Ronald, helped raise us after my father passed away. He has always been such a positive role model to me, because of all the things he sacrificed to become the man of the house at the age of thirteen. My brother, Romont, was the wild child growing up. For a long time, I just did the opposite of everything he would do, because that would help me avoid getting hit by my mother. When they talk about older brothers beating up their younger brothers, he was the one who would deliver the beat downs to <u>me</u>. I always had a wisecrack or two (maybe even three); and, he was always twice my size. It ended up being a very bad combination. But, it made me tough; and, I learned how to start picking my battles. For example, when mom was home, I could talk crap to Romont; but, when mom was at work, I would lock myself in my room and pray that Romont wouldn't remember that I had talked crap to him the day before.

My sister was the baby. So, one of the early things I learned from her, when I was growing up, was that outside of the President, she was the next closest person to being 'untouchable'. Mess with her; and, mom would deliver the message of a lifetime. Testing that theory was a painful lesson (which had to be taught to me ONLY a FEW Times – Thank God!). As you can see, my childhood was never boring. We grew up in some tough situations; but, we were able to handle them. One of the hardest situations for me to comprehend as a child was dealing with my older brother Craig, who is autistic.

In this picture, Craig is the one with his finger resting on his temple which is his famous *"Thinker"* pose. When I was younger, I knew Craig was *"different"*. I had no idea as to what autism was; and, my mom never really brought it up. Back then, words like *"retarded"* were used for anyone who wasn't considered *"normal"*. Thinking back on it now, I still can't believe how accepted that word was in regards to someone who was considered mentally-handicapped. Craig is my second-oldest, full-blood brother. His autism was always a mystery to me. He would talk to himself from time to time – or had to shake hands with everyone in church – and, for the life of me, I couldn't understand why.

I would get embarrassed, when Craig would walk into the store going a million-miles-per-hour and people would stare at us and whisper to themselves. I remember when I was a teenager working at a pharmacy. My mom dropped by; and, Craig came in like a tornado, walking around the store talking to himself. A couple in the aisle where my register was located started snickering. I stood there and didn't say a word. I felt REALLY embarrassed. And, to this day, I still get mad at myself for not giving those two morons a piece of my mind.

Autism made Craig do some things that were 'abnormal' to most people; but, it also gave him the ability to do some extraordinary things, as well. To this day, Craig is one of the best spellers I have ever met. When we were young, all we had to do is say a word and Craig could spell it. It didn't matter what the word was; and, he didn't need it in a sentence. Craig became my spellchecker, before that option was available. Most people who know me say I have an above-average memory. – But, Craig's memory makes me feel like I have some type of severe amnesia.

Right now, Craig is into collecting records from the 50's, 60's, and 70's. If someone mentions a song title from any of those years, Craig can tell you the artist, the year the record was produced, and anything else you wanted to know about the song. It's his 'gift'; and, it's truly amazing to see it in action. Craig loves music. It's definitely one of the things we have in common. When I go to my mom's house, I'll watch Craig break down some 'old school' dance moves while listening to Stevie Wonder or Al Green. (If any of you folks don't know who these people are, shame on you!) Craig literally stole the show at my wedding. Any dance circle that formed was immediately filled with him doing his moves. We're cut from the same cloth. It doesn't matter if there's no one else on the dance floor or if it's crowded, when music comes on we're out there.

While growing up, Craig never really showed a lot of emotion. When my mom used to give us spankings, Craig would always be outside the door laughing. My brothers and I used to get so mad, until my mom told us the story as to why he laughs. When my father was alive, Craig used to cry so much when my older brother got spanked – that my dad basically told him to cut it out or he'd get one too. So, laughing was his way of not crying. When I first moved out of my mom's house and into my apartment, I was happy to be closer to my job and my friends, etc. Melissa had just moved in and we were hanging out one night, when I got a phone call. The call was from Craig. I almost had a heart attack. In all my years on this earth, Craig had never called anyone (including me). We talked about music for a couple of minutes; and, then he let me go. When I told my mom about the conversation, she was in shock (just as I had been). A couple of days later, the same thing happened. My other brothers were jealous, since Craig had never called them. – Craig missed me; and, that was his way of letting me know.

Craig is four years older than I am and still looks really young. A couple of years ago, he had a scare regarding his heart. We had to take him to the hospital a couple of times, and I'll never forget looking at him in the hospital bed. All Craig cared about is what was on the television. All of us were scared for him; and, yet, he didn't really have a care in the world. On my way home, I tried to imagine not having him in my life (and couldn't do it without my eyes watering up).

We tend to dismiss what we don't understand. When people are *"different"*, we forget that they are still just people. Craig's life lesson to me has been to "Just Be Yourself!" and don't care if you get a funny look every once in a while. All that really matters is that you're happy!

ABOUT THE AUTHOR

ACKNOWLEDGEMENTS

I would like to first thank my mother Tina Thomas for teaching me the life lessons I needed to not only survive but thrive in this world. I would like to thank my beautiful wife Melissa for her support through thick and thin, and for our son Bryce who one day will make footprints of his own. I would like to thank my siblings Robert, Ronald,Tony,Craig,Romont,Alicia, and Jackie for always being there for me through childhood and now as an adult. My west coast mom Janice Mitchell who has welcomed me into her family with open arms. All my aunts, uncles and family that have shown me love throughout my life. My cousin Carlos for inspiring me to pick up a basketball. My Crossroads Basketball family which covers over two hundred people, I love you all for believing in what we do and how we do it. Joe Mantegna and my Blair Academy family. The wonderful people at Oola for inspiring me daily and penning such a great forward. Alan Stein, China Smith, Brett Timmons, Hugh Shields, and Maria Giacalone for all her help in the process. Sinclair, Ntellekt, Impowerr, Alex and Ani, Mia Praught, Mia, Mona Berberich and the better weekdays family, Annie Hawkins, Les Floyd, Emily Thomas, Jason Houck, Tracey Edwards, and all my great friends that help spread the word through social media. Joey P for helping me start my first blog. The Stafford family, Hayes family, Kniffin family, Cavanaugh Family, Feltus Family, Korn Family, Lord Family, Ledesma Family, Faubert Family, Muller Family, Goldsberry Family, Real World Family, Renzo Gracie Family, Snyder Family, Baranowski Family, Abrahamsen Family, DeMasi Family, Breheny Family,

Smith Family, Livingston Family, Pinsonault Family, D'Alessio family, Synol Family, Jackson Family, Endicott family, and countless others that have helped me throughout this process. A special thanks to Kristen Rath photography for their unbelievable work and patience on the cover, and author photo. This page wouldn't be complete if I didn't save the last spot for my two fathers. Bobby Thomas despite only being alive for my first four years on earth, you have inspired me throughout my life with the countless stories of how much you gave back to the community of Passaic, and to those less fortunate. Your footprints are too big to follow so I will do my best to walk right next to them. My second dad Steve Mitchell, a real life cowboy in every since of the word. You accepted me with open arms and gave me your blessing to marry your daughter. I know the two of you are smiling down at your grandson Bryce, I love you with all my heart.

Made in the USA
Charleston, SC
11 October 2013